Mapping My Day

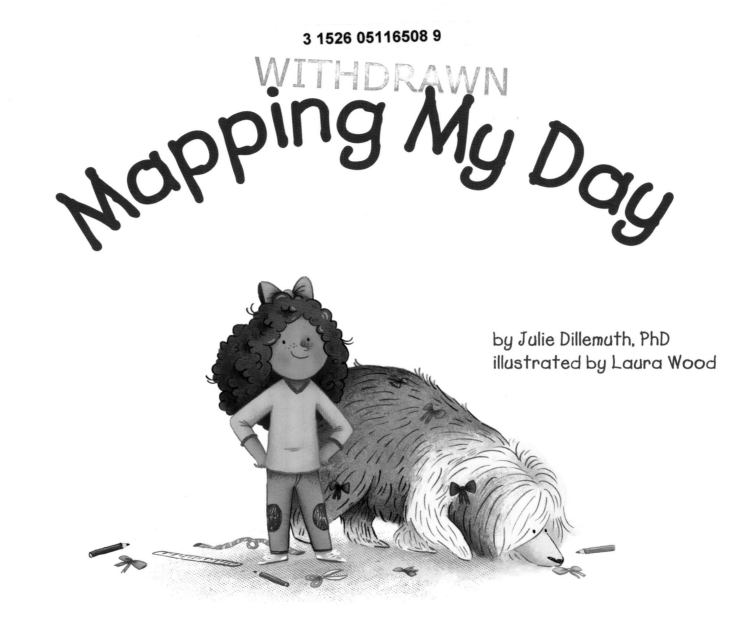

by Julie Dillemuth, PhD
illustrated by Laura Wood

Magination Press • Washington, DC • American Psychological Association

Published by
MAGINATION PRESS®
An Educational Publishing Foundation Book
American Psychological Association
750 First Street NE
Washington, DC 20002

Magination Press is a registered trademark of the American Psychological Association.

For more information about our books, including a complete catalog, please write to us, call 1-800-374-2721, or visit our website at www.apa.org/pubs/magination.

Book design by Gwen Grafft
Printed by Phoenix Color Corporation, Hagerstown, MD

Library of Congress Cataloging-in-Publication Data

Names: Dillemuth, Julie, author. | Wood, Laura, 1985- illustrator.
Title: Mapping my day / by Julie Dillemuth ; illustrated by Laura Wood.
Description: Washington, DC : Magination Press, [2017] | "American
    Psychological Association." | Summary: "A little girl loves drawing maps
    — of her buried treasure, the breakfast table, the route to school, and
    more — taking the reader on a journey through her day; a story told in
    maps. This book inspires readers to create their own maps and diagrams,
    gaining practice in making drawings with meaningful spatial relationships.
    Includes note to parents and mapping activities"— Provided by publisher.
Identifiers: LCCN 2016024409 | ISBN 9781433823336 (hardcover) |
    ISBN 1433823330 (hardcover)
Subjects: | CYAC: Maps — Fiction.
Classification: LCC PZ7.1.D56 Map 2017 | DDC [E] — dc23 LC record
    available at https://lccn.loc.gov/2016024409

Manufactured in the United States of America
10 9 8 7 6 5 4 3 2 1

My day begins with the sun…in my face.
The sun rises in the east, so guess which direction
my bedroom window faces?

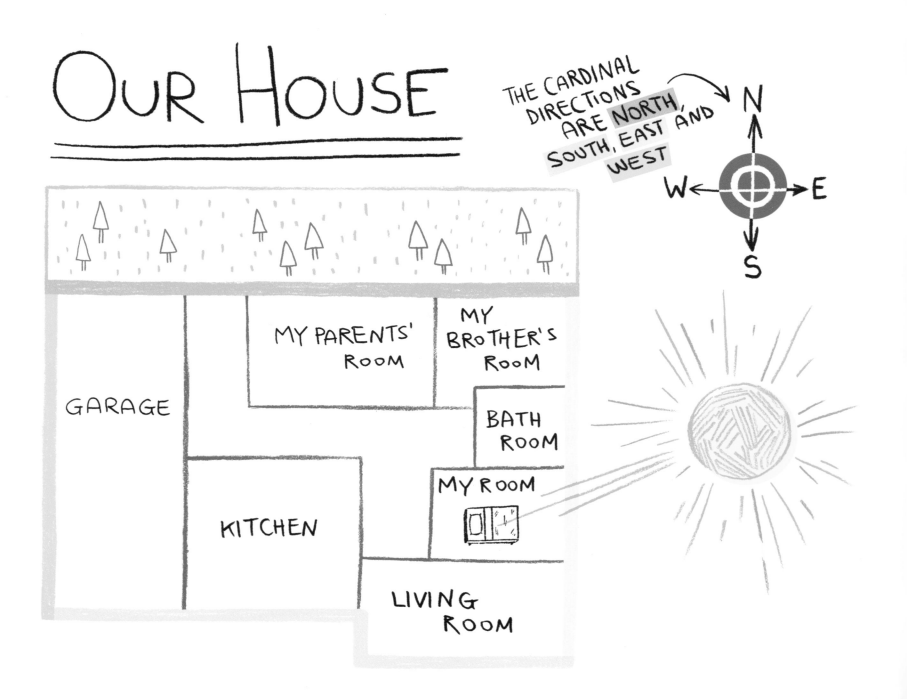

That's how I learned the
cardinal directions so early.
Too early, if you ask me.

When I hear my brother's door open,
I bolt to the bathroom to get there first. And I can because…

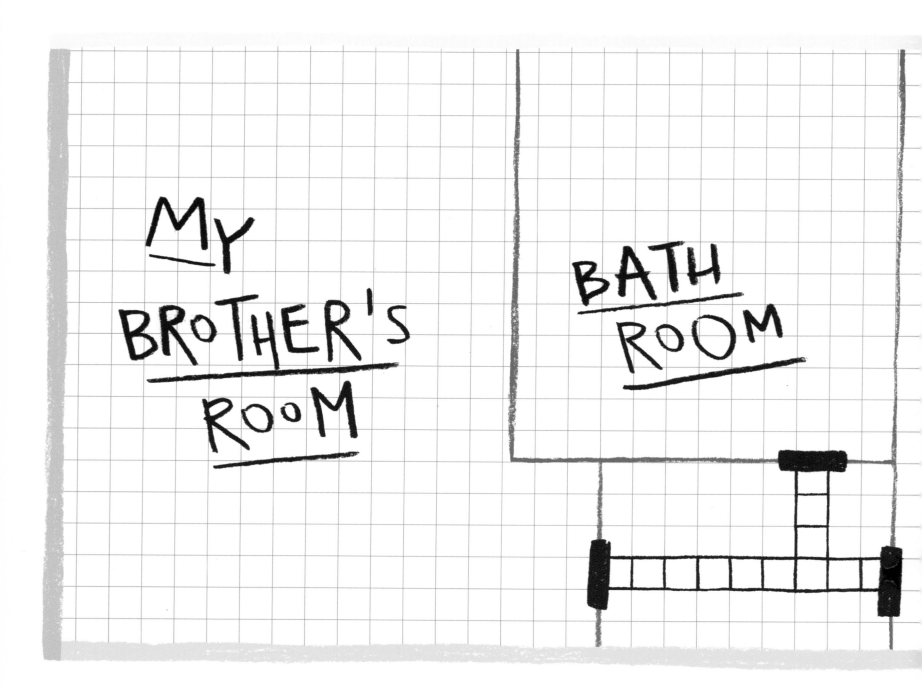

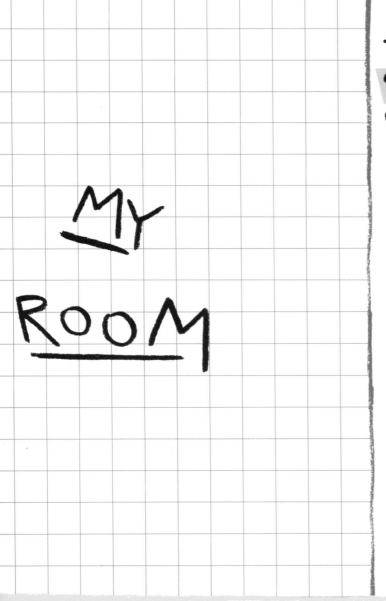

MY ROOM

THE MAP SCALE SHOWS YOU HOW TO MEASURE.

☐ = 1 Step

IN THIS MAP, ONE SQUARE IS EQUAL TO ONE STEP —

COUNT THEM UP!

…my room is four steps closer to the bathroom than his. This map is **to scale**, so you can see exactly how many steps closer my bedroom is.

Today before breakfast I need to use my secret treasure map.
My brother keeps stealing my fancy hair bows, so they are going into
my treasure chest! This is how I got started making maps in the first place.

I found a treasure chest box in the garage one day and filled it with my most special things. I picked a spot in the back yard and buried it, but I needed a map to remember how to find it again. My brother tried to find my treasure once, but he didn't have the map. After digging five holes around the yard, Dad got mad and made him stop.

To find my treasure you need
to know exactly how far to go
from the biggest tree in the yard.
Starting there, you walk
seven steps east, then three steps
southeast. 'X' marks the spot!

THE BIGGEST TREE
IS A LANDMARK,
OR A ONE-OF-A-KIND
THING THAT STANDS OUT

We all eat breakfast together every day.
Aunt June is visiting, and she's pretty big
so Mom put her where I normally sit.
We added an extra chair, and I have to
squeeze in next to my brother. You'd
think this would be annoying, but…

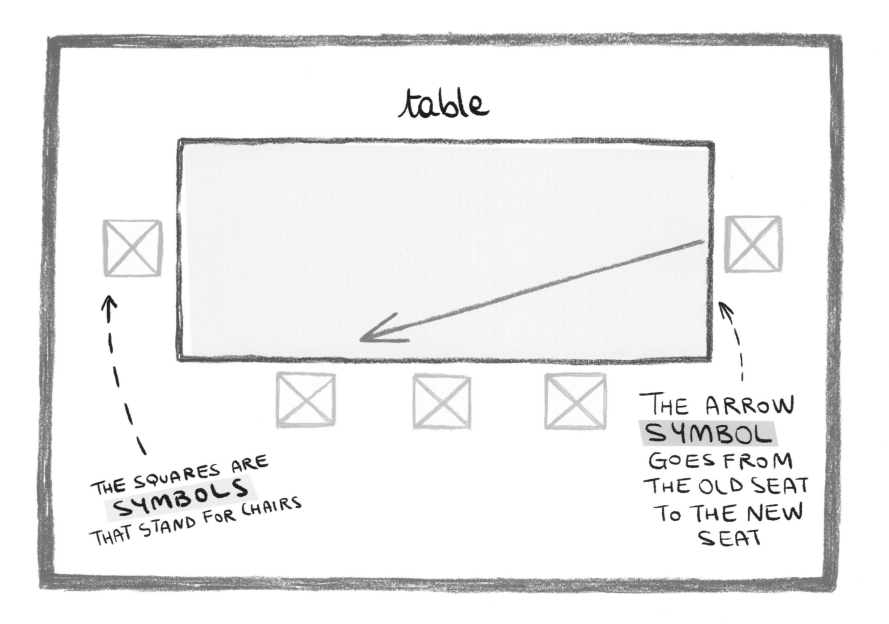

table

THE SQUARES ARE **SYMBOLS** THAT STAND FOR CHAIRS

THE ARROW **SYMBOL** GOES FROM THE OLD SEAT TO THE NEW SEAT

...I can whisper funny things to him
until he snorts milk out his nose,
without getting in trouble.

Then, it's off to school. When Dad drives, we go straight through town.

But Mom hates traffic lights, so when she drives we go a longer way that has only one light. It actually takes the same amount of time.

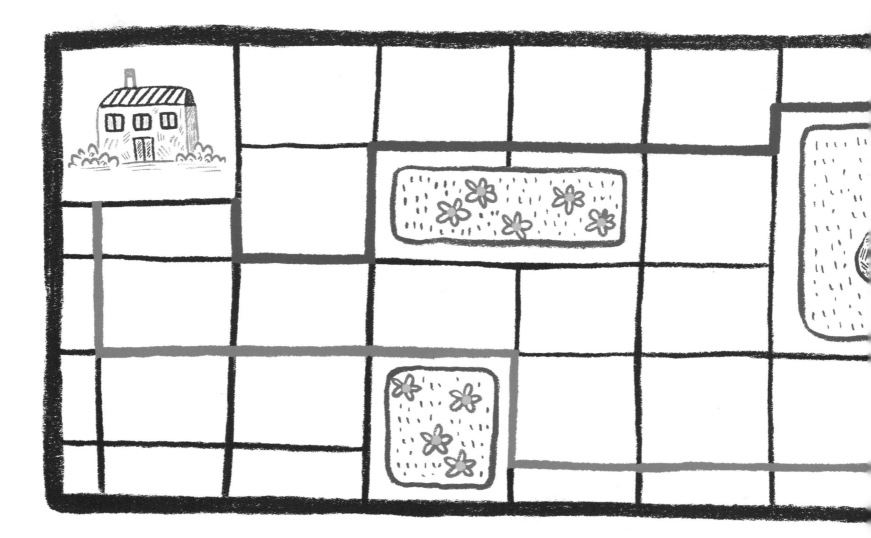

Dad's **route** and Mom's are in different colors to tell them apart. I also drew in my favorite **landmark**, the cow on top of McCorkel's ice cream factory.

THE LEGEND → SHOWS YOU WHICH ROUTE IS WHICH

mom's Route
dad's Route

The playground is my favorite place at school.
And the slide is my favorite thing on the playground.

But, remember that the sun rises in the *east*?
Well, it sets in the *west*, which means trouble at the slide.

legend

:·. maple tree seeds

shade

N
W—E
S

Look at all that shade *northeast* of the trees. But the slide is too far *south*, and it faces *west*—right into the sun! By afternoon recess the slide is baking in the sun, and it burns my legs!

I buried a bunch of maple tree seeds to make more shade, but they aren't growing fast enough. Where are Jack's magic beans when you need them?

Can you guess where I planted the tree seeds? Look at the cardinal directions on the compass rose. Hint: to make shade, they need to go between the sun and the slide. Did you guess right? The legend tells you that the green dots show where the seeds are planted.

After school we go to my Grandma's for a few hours. She has an agility course in her backyard—that's an obstacle course for dogs. Her poodle Priscilla wins all kinds of competitions. When my brother and I play agility dog show, I usually do all the winning. Unless Priscilla plays with us.

The course is tricky because you have to do everything in just the right order.

Back at home, we have dinner, I do my homework, and then it's time for bed.
Sometimes I go to amazing places in my dreams. I'll draw a map of them for you…

tomorrow.

Note to Parents, Caregivers, and Professionals

In this book, the main character, Flora, loves drawing, especially drawing maps. Beyond showing where things are, maps reveal spatial relationships: where things and places are in relation to other things. Maps tell stories and convey information. As we read this book, each of the maps or diagrams illustrates something Flora wants to tell us about her life.

By the time we're adults, most of us have seen a variety of maps and diagrams and have practice (though maybe not proficiency!) reading information from them. For kids or anyone without much experience with maps, interpreting maps and diagrams is usually challenging and confusing, and prone to error. This book helps with foundational map interpretation in that for each scene in the story, we first see a regular illustrated picture of what is happening, followed by a map of the same thing on the next page. Comparing what's on the map to what's happening in the picture can help readers figure out the story in the map or diagram.

For readers of all ages, the three goals of this book are to:

1) Show readers that maps can convey many types of information. Maps can tell all sorts of stories, sometimes more easily than with words.

2) Inspire kids to draw their own maps and diagrams. Drawing spatial relationships is an excellent way to develop this spatial skill, and understanding spatial relationships is important for many aspects of life, including math and science learning.

3) Introduce basic map concepts and vocabulary, and demonstrate why they are important. Each map in the story highlights just one or two map concepts at a time (compass rose, scale bar, legend, etc.), which are necessary for understanding that particular map.

Children as young as preschool age can start learning about maps and diagrams. Gaining proficiency in making and using these visual tools will set them up for success later in school (in science and math, in particular) and in everyday life. Plus, many kids find maps fun and want to incorporate them in their play.

Map Concepts and Activities

The following are some ideas for activities you can do with children to reinforce the concepts from this book and take them further. If you are a teacher, these activities are easily adapted for the classroom.

Drawing

Maps and diagrams are pictures specifically of spatial relationships. But any drawing involves decisions about space and spatial relationships—where the drawing is on the paper, how big it is, how different parts of the drawing relate to each other, etc. Encourage your child to have fun with drawing. It doesn't matter what they choose to draw, whether abstract shapes or detailed scenes—the main thing is to enjoy it and have fun.

Tell a story with a map. In this book, Flora draws maps and diagrams to tell us about her day. See if you and your child can tell each other stories with a map, diagram, or spatial picture that you draw.

Play "I Spy" by drawing. Choose something in the room for your child to guess. With paper and pencil or crayons, draw the object you're thinking of, and keep drawing until your child guesses correctly. Then it's your child's turn to choose something to draw. (Younger kids may need some help getting started with the drawing. You could suggest they start with its basic shape, or use crayons to give a clue with the color.)

Cardinal Directions and Compass Rose

The compass rose tells you which direction is which on a map. Many maps are oriented so that north is "up." In this book, Flora is tuned in to the directions since the sun rising in the east shines into her eyes every morning. She also uses cardinal directions to explain the bad planning at the school playground, which left the slide in the sun, not in the shade.

Make a compass. An internet search for "make a compass" will turn up lots of sites and videos with instructions on making a compass, as well as the science behind how a compass works. Make one with your child, then do fun things like figure out which direction the bedroom window faces, just like Flora did.

Follow directions. When you and your child go to school, figure out the general direction you go to get there and the individual directions of the streets you take. Regular practice will help children get a better sense of the cardinal directions in their mental maps.

Scale Bar
A scale bar on a map lets you measure distances. Sometimes it's helpful or important to be able to measure distance, to get a sense of how far away something is or when you want to figure out how long it will take to get somewhere. Flora used a map drawn to scale to figure out that her room was closer to the bathroom than her brother's. She also used it for her treasure map.

Measure a map. Find a map, either paper or digital (such as from Google Maps), and help your child use the scale bar to measure some distances. Find your neighborhood and figure out how long your block is, or add up the distance from home to school or some other place that's important to your child. You could also figure out which playground, toy store, library, etc. is closest to your house compared to others.

Compare distances. Use graph paper or the Activity Page at the end of this book to make a map like Flora did to compare

distances between things. Each square is one unit of measure, which can be a formal measure, like a meter, or something easy like the length of your child's step. With your child, think about what might be fun to measure and compare. For example, if there are different ways to get to a place in your house or yard, figure out which way takes fewer steps.

Build to scale. Take the activity above to three dimensions and build something to scale. Use Legos, blocks, magnetic tiles, or any favorite building material to create a scale model of your child's room, your house, or whatever inspires your child. Measure the dimensions using your child's steps, a meter stick, or a ruler, then decide how much distance a block, brick, or tile represents.

Landmarks
A landmark is something that stands out and is unique (so that you can't confuse it with something else) that helps you orient yourself in your surroundings. We look out for landmarks when we go places or give directions. Flora's favorite landmark is a statue of a cow on top of the nearby ice cream factory.

Make a landmark scavenger hunt. What interesting landmarks can you identify where you live? Make a list and see if your child can recognize them. You can do this sitting still, using your mental maps and drawing or describing where they are, or you can take a drive or a walk and let your child navigate you to the landmarks on the list.

Create imaginary maps. Does your child pretend the backyard or school playground is some other place—a kingdom, a fortress, a magical land? Suggest that they draw a map of it, complete with landmarks. It could even end up being a treasure map or an enchanted map with magical powers to become part of the game.

Symbols

Symbols are everywhere, from school zone street signs to restroom signs, and we often take for granted what they mean. A symbol is a simple picture or shape that represents something and conveys a meaning. On maps, symbols don't take up a lot of space, which is important when a small map represents a big area, or lots of things need to fit on a piece of paper or smartphone screen.

Guess the symbols. Grab some paper and pencils, make up your own symbols, and take turns guessing what they mean. A fork and spoon for a restaurant, a slide for a playground, or a book for the library are some examples. Think about your child's favorite places and things for inspiration.

Design your own symbols. Enlist your child's help to "get organized" and label where things go in the house with symbols instead of words. Use sticky notes or bits of paper with non-marking tape for drawing the symbol labels—in your child's room, a book could symbolize the bookshelves, a coat hanger for the closet, symbols for the type of clothing in each dresser drawer, etc.

Legend

A legend lists the symbols on a map along with their meaning. Often, we recognize what the symbols mean and don't need to refer to the legend, but if we're unfamiliar with the symbols, then the legend is key.

Map your symbols. In conjunction with the Design Your Own Symbols activity above, make a map that includes everything for which you made a symbol, and draw a legend on it that explains the symbols.

Find real-world examples. Legends are essential on maps from places like theme-parks, zoos, and museums. Plan or reminisce about a trip by poring over one of these maps and finding favorite attractions (most maps are available on the venue's website, or when you're there, pick up a paper version). Transportation maps can also be fun—try it with bus, train, or subway maps from your area.

Route

A route on a map shows you how to get from one place to another. In this age of digital maps and smartphones with navigation apps, we encounter routes on maps all the time.

Find the routes. Look at a map that includes your neighborhood and your child's school, and together figure out how many different ways you can get from your house to school. Talk about why you go the way that you do. Look up maps of other familiar areas, either online, such as with Google Maps, or on a paper map.

Map out a walk. Plan a walk or a hike somewhere nearby, and print out or draw a map of the route you plan to take. You can even include the cardinal directions by drawing a compass rose. Have your child follow along the map as you walk. You can help your child rotate the map as you make turns, to match the direction you're walking (note that some people like to do this, while others prefer to keep the map in a fixed orientation).

Plan for an emergency. Does your family or school have an emergency plan for where you go in the event of a fire or other emergency? Draw a map together with escape routes or shelters, and make sure everyone knows where to go in an emergency (your child can play Fire Marshall and explain the map to the grown-ups). When you stay in a hotel, help your child study the map on the back of the door that shows the emergency escape routes. This is both good map-reading practice (especially if you yourself are easily disoriented in hotels) and good safety practice!

Enjoy these activities or make up your own, but most of all, keep it fun! You or your child may find some of these suggestions challenging, and that's okay. Go at your own pace, and feel free to modify any of the activities to fit your situation. Even without doing additional activities, simply reading this book with your child will make both of you more aware of the value of drawing and thinking about spatial relationships.

Draw Your Own Map!

Use the space below to draw a map. It could be a map of your house, your room, your school or classroom, your favorite playground, or another special place. Can you tell a story with your map?

Map Legend Mix-Up

This legend is all mixed up! Sort it out by matching up the symbols from the story with the words that mean the same thing. Draw a line between the pairs that match.

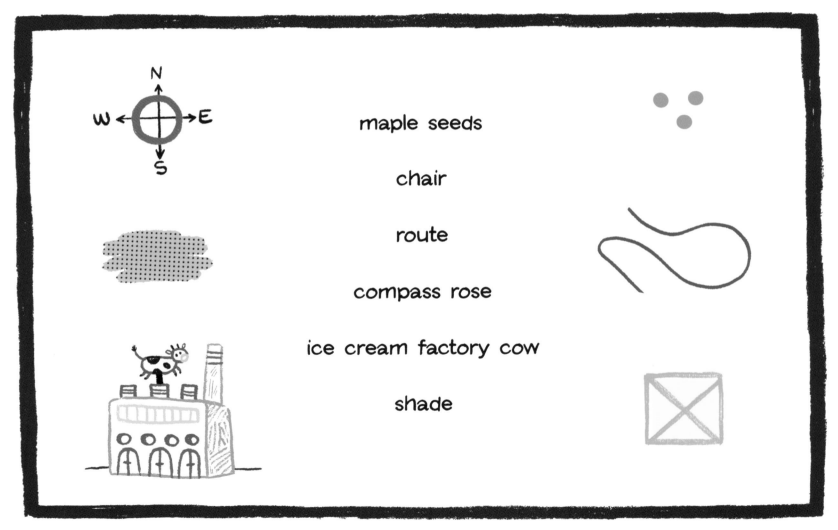

maple seeds

chair

route

compass rose

ice cream factory cow

shade

Trace the Route

Help Flora get to the library by tracing a route on the map. The lines represent sidewalks, and you can make up any route you want to get her there. If she wants to stop at the playground on the way home, how should she go?

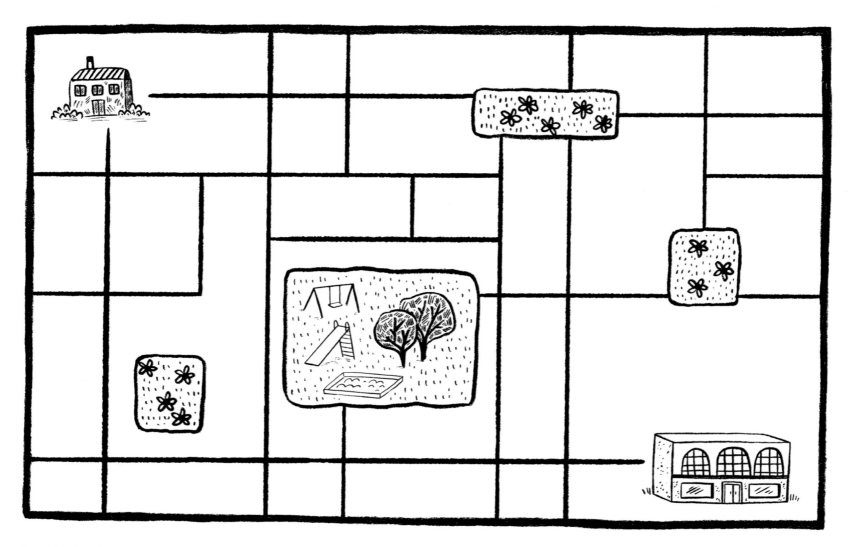

Compare Distances

Make a map like Flora did to compare distances between things. Each square is one unit of measurement, which can be one step, five steps, the length of a meter stick, or anything else you decide. What would be fun to measure and compare? One idea is, if there are different ways to get to a place in your house or yard, figure out which way takes fewer steps.

THE MAP SCALE SHOWS YOU HOW TO MEASURE.

☐ =

About the Author

Julie Dillemuth, PhD, was mystified by maps until she figured out how to read them and make them, and it was a particularly difficult map that inspired her to become a spatial cognition geographer. She writes children's books in Santa Barbara, California, where the west coast faces south. Contact her at juliedillemuth.com.

About the Illustrator

Laura Wood is an independent illustrator currently living in the wonderful city of Bristol, UK. Her work can be found in picture books, educational publications, and digital apps as well as editorial publications. By day, she spends her time in her studio bringing stories to life. By night, she likes to put on her dancing shoes and swing dance under the stars. She is proudly represented by the lovely people at Good Illustration Agency.

About Magination Press

Magination Press is an imprint of the American Psychological Association, the largest scientific and professional organization representing psychologists in the United States and the largest association of psychologists worldwide.